—— Careers for Creative People ——

Careers in Film, TV, and Theater

Don Nardo

ReferencePoint
Press®

San Diego, CA

© 2020 ReferencePoint Press, Inc.
Printed in the United States

For more information, contact:
ReferencePoint Press, Inc.
PO Box 27779
San Diego, CA 92198
www.ReferencePointPress.com

LIBRARY OF CONGRESS CATALOGING-IN-PUBLICATION DATA

Name: Nardo, Don, 1947– author.
Title: Careers in Film, TV, and Theater/by Don Nardo.
Description: San Diego, CA: ReferencePoint Press, Inc., 2020. | Series: Careers for Creative People series | Audience: Grades 9-12. | Includes bibliographical references and index.
Identifiers: LCCN 2019004313 (print) | LCCN 2019009344 (ebook) | ISBN 9781682826829 (eBook) | ISBN 9781682826812 | ISBN 9781682826812¬(hardback)
Subjects: LCSH: Motion pictures—Vocational guidance—Juvenile literature. | Television—Vocational guidance—Juvenile literature. | Theater—Vocational guidance—Juvenile literature.
Classification: LCC PN1995.9.P75 (ebook) | LCC PN1995.9.P75 N37 2020 (print) | DDC 791.4302/3—dc23
LC record available at https://lccn.loc.gov/2019004313

Contents

Creating Magic Onstage and in Film

The great nineteenth-century Irish playwright Oscar Wilde once said, "I love acting. It's so much more real than life." This was his way of saying that acting is a supremely expressive and creative profession. In fact, Wilde believed that actors are among the most creative people in society, an opinion with which the majority of people would still readily agree more than a century later. "Creativity can be defined as the ability to produce something of value that did not exist before," writes Dennis Vilorio, a researcher for the Bureau of Labor Statistics, in a June 2015 article for the bureau's Career Outlook web publication. In his view, an actor is creative because he or she fashions a unique, never-before-seen character and brings it to life for an audience.

Like many people, in his own day and now, when Wilde thought about the theater and its creative artists, he initially thought of actors—after all, they are the most visible people in that entertainment venue. The same remains true of the two illustrious offshoots of the theater—films and television. Yet Wilde was aware that there is much more to the theater than merely actors and their craft. Backing up the actors is a small army of equally creative artists and craftspeople of many different types. The words the theater actors speak are penned by a playwright, for instance, and their movements onstage are choreographed by a director. Meanwhile, a costume designer fashions the clothes the actors wear, and a set decorator fabricates the environments they pretend to inhabit.

Film and Television Equivalents

In the early twentieth century, motion pictures—more commonly called movies or films—inherited these highly creative occupations and many more that had long made staging plays possible. Moreover, the same thing happened when television, or TV for short, began to thrive in the late 1940s and early 1950s. Both film and television productions routinely feature not only actors but also their equivalent of playwrights—screenwriters—along with directors, costume designers, and many others.

There *are* some notable differences between live theater and filmed drama. For example, theater actors generally do their own makeup and hair, whereas in films and TV productions, these areas are handled by professionals who specialize in them—makeup artists and hairstylists. Like so many other jobs in theater and film, that of makeup artists is highly creative. In part this is because they design and execute something artistic from scratch. This ability to create something that did not exist before is part of the intrinsic magic of theater and film. Legendary Oscar-winning makeup artist for movies and TV Rick Baker explains it well. "For most of my career I've been really hands-on," he says in a Pixologic interview. "I design the characters and sculpt the stuff and apply the makeups and paint it and put hair on it and do all that kind of stuff. Now, more than anything, it's design work."

Similarly, if a play calls for a stage actor to fall down or throw a punch, he or she does it live, in real time. In comparison, in movies and on TV, those and other potentially dangerous moves are performed by professional stuntpeople. The filmic equivalent of theatrical set decorators, meanwhile, are art directors, often called production designers. Working under the production designer are various set decorators and prop makers and procurers.

There are also numerous jobs connected to a device not seen in the theater but fundamental to films and TV—the motion picture camera. In consultation with the director, the cinematographer (or director of photography) oversees the overall look of the visuals the camera captures. The cinematographer's crew usually includes several camera operators and lighting experts.

Many Opportunities Available

The theater, film, and television jobs described above represent only a small portion of the many creative occupations that make these major entertainment venues possible. Any of those professions is in reach of whoever has enough time, talent, and personal ambition and dedication to pursue it. The making of a single feature film, for example, relies on the work of hundreds of people, the popular website All About Careers explains:

> Behind the final cut of every flick on the big screen is a dedicated team of people who must work incredibly hard throughout the entire process of creating the motion picture. A ton of opportunities are available to you in the exciting world of film. You might [work] within the music department, become a stunt professional, or work as a special effects expert, just to make it all that extra bit magical.

Whether someone wants to be part of the magic that appears on large or small screens or the magic created onstage for live audiences, he or she is confronted by two general choices. One is to rely on talent and instincts alone; the other is to acquire some sort of schooling. Although there is no right or wrong choice, most experts favor going to school. If the desired occupation is in the film industry, for example, the website Careers in Film argues for learning "your craft quickly and from experts. Also, surrounding yourself with others who have the same passions and goals as you do is powerful. It creates momentum." Overall, the site says, "attending a school or college can really propel your career in film."

Taking the school route is not a guarantee of success, however. As can be the case in almost any career, Vilorio points out,

Occupation	Minimum Educational Requirement	2017 Median Pay
Actor	Some college, no degree	$17.49 per hour
Advertising, promotion, and marketing manager	Bachelor's degree	$129,380
Carpenter	High school diploma or equivalent	$45,170
Electrician	High school diploma or equivalent	$54,110
Fashion designer	Bachelor's degree	$67,420
Film and video editor, and camera operator	Bachelor's degree	$58,210
Hairstylist and cosmetologist	Postsecondary non-degree	$24,900
Multimedia artist and animator	Bachelor's degree	$70,530
Producer and director	Bachelor's degree	$71,620
Writer and author	Bachelor's degree	$61,820

Source: Bureau of Labor Statistics, *Occupational Outlook Handbook*, 2019. www.bls.gov.

"creative workers may face challenges in their jobs that they need to overcome. To succeed, they must be able to handle stress and frustration, accept criticism and failure, and learn to persevere." Nevertheless, virtually all who have managed to work for at least a while in theater, films, or television will attest that doing whatever is necessary to overcome the inevitable challenges is well worth it in the long run.

Theatrical Dancer

What Does a Theatrical Dancer Do?

Like actors and singers, dancers are on the front line of musical theater, both on and off Broadway. A Broadway show is generally defined as a stage production presented in one of the roughly forty theaters each having five hundred or more seats in New York City's theater district. Broadway is generally viewed as one of the two most distinguished theater hubs in the world, the other being London's main theater district. Virtually all musicals feature at least a few dancers, and some employ dozens of them. Each musical production has a choreographer who designs the dance routines to go with the composer's music and teaches those routines to the dancers.

Most often the dancing is a visual expression of various ideas, themes, or events within the story told in the musical play. Once the dancers have learned the steps and routines, they are expected to repeat them precisely throughout a musical's run, which might encompass as few as three or as many as hundreds of performances.

At a Glance

Theatrical Dancer

Minimum Educational Requirements
None, but most dancers take numerous dance and movement classes

Personal Qualities
Physical strength and agility, willingness to work hard, dedication

Working Conditions
Mostly working in dance studios and rehearsal halls in the daytime and theaters in the evenings

Salary Range
From $500 to $1,754 per week in 2018

Number of Jobs
About 6,000 to 7,000 in 2016

Future Job Outlook
Growth of 4 percent through 2026*

*Includes dancers and choreographers

Theatrical dancers might be expected to know and perform highly varied dance styles. These can range from classical ballet moves to all manner of modern ones, from jazz to ethnic varieties. Moreover, the dancers are often expected to do more than dance. For example, the most successful professional dancers also have solid singing voices and even acting "chops" (or skills). In an interview on the website of *Dance Informa* magazine, successful Broadway dancer Diane Laurenson explains:

> It is your responsibility, your job, to come to work eight shows a week and perform to the fullest. As in any other exceptional performance situation, you are among an elite few who are expected to give it all every night. Eat well, get plenty of rest, continue studying and growing and make every move important. And last but not least, a step is a step is a step is a boring step. Dance the *emotion*, dance the *idea*, dance the *story* and *character*, dance the *music*! People who practice this perform on a higher level—a Broadway-caliber level. One mustn't *want* to perform, one must *need* to perform.

This mini lecture to professional dancers effectively captures the reality that being a dancer is less about flashy routines and audience and applause and more about good old-fashioned sweat and hard work.

How Do You Become a Theatrical Dancer?

Education

Formal training in the form of dance classes essential for a successful career as a theatrical dancer, especially for those dancers who aspire to perform in New York City, in London, or on road shows (touring shows) that are cast and rehearsed in those premier theater hubs. Some beginning dancers choose to study dance in college, and a number of American colleges have excellent dance programs. A few of the best include New York University, the University of Arizona, Bryn Mawr College, Fordham University, Boston University, and Florida State University. Other young dancers train instead at private dance schools, which can be found in several big US cities, especially New York City, the home of Broadway.

Even after graduating from a dance school, however, a theatrical dancer's training and education have only just begun. He or she should continue to take some sort of classes for years to come. These not only keep a person in good physical shape and limber but also allow him or her to learn new dance steps and practice older ones. As veteran dancer Victoria Dombroski puts it in an article for *Backstage* magazine posted online,

> There is never an excuse to not take class. At all hours of the day, you can find almost any class of your choosing at one of the main dance studios in NYC. Whether you need to brush up those tap skills or get your ballet technique back in serious shape, you should take advantage of all the options the city has to offer!

Musical theater dance coach Trish Causey agrees and advises that if a young dancer can afford to pursue only one style of dance, he or she should opt for ballet. "Ballet is the foundation of Broadway dance," she explains in an article for the website Majoring in Music. "Ballet training is absolutely necessary for working in musical theatre because choreography is given using French terms from ballet, which you must know at auditions and rehearsals."

Causey's mention of auditions is crucial because attending auditions for dancing jobs is also part of a professional dancer's essential training. With extremely rare exceptions, even the most talented dancers do not walk into their first, second, or even tenth audition and get hired. In fact, most professionals report having to attend as many as one hundred or more auditions before getting their first job.

Another tip to beginners from veteran dancers and choreographers is not to rely only on classes, dance practice, and auditions to learn the craft. All professional dancers agree that much can be learned simply from watching the greats of prior generations.

Dancers practice in preparation for a performance. Throughout their careers, theatrical dancers are continually learning new steps, practicing familiar ones, and just generally working to keep their bodies strong and agile.

In Causey's words, "Watch movie musicals from the 'Golden Age' of Broadway and Hollywood. Rent or download movies produced by MGM, RKO, and 20th Century Fox . . . [to] gain knowledge, understanding, and appreciation of the musical as a living art form."

Volunteer Work and Internships

Various dance companies and schools across the United States offer chances for young dancers, often children, to perform onstage in small parts or crowd scenes. Most often, these opportunities roughly mirror the apprentice program run by the Boston Ballet; it has a school for young dancers, and the most skilled of these unpaid apprentices are chosen to take part in performances of *The Nutcracker* during the Christmas season. (The children most often play mice or fairies, parts that do not require professional-level dancing skills.) The Boston Ballet also has yearly programs for unpaid interns in their late teens or twenties.

Although such positions usually consist of administrative functions, the interns get to be around and benefit from advice from professional dancers.

Skills and Personality

Professional theatrical dancers should first and foremost acquire basic ballet training. They also need to become proficient in a wide variety of more modern dance styles, including jazz, tap, standard ballroom (waltz, fox-trot, rumba, cha-cha, and so forth), ethnic styles of various kinds, hip-hop, and others. Many veteran dancers and dance teachers also recommend acquiring basic gymnastics skills, which improve both balance and the ability to leap high into the air.

In addition, most modern dancers now take singing and acting classes when possible, mainly because the producers and directors of most Broadway, off-Broadway, and road-show musicals look for chorus members who are a so-called triple threat (that is, someone who can dance, sing, and act). As a result, many young dancers prepare audition material that displays all these skills.

Regarding personality, a successful theatrical dancer tends to be willing to work extremely hard and to sacrifice many comforts for long periods of time to achieve his or her goals. A dancer requires the ability to take repeated rejection without becoming completely discouraged and giving up on his or her dream. One observer of the professional dance scene, Lisa Magloff, effectively sums up the sometimes harsh reality of what it takes to become a successful theatrical dancer in an article for the website Bizfluent. "This is an extremely competitive field," she says, "and dancers often train day and night for years before they can begin to audition for Broadway shows."

On the Job

Employers

Theatrical dancers work in several different venues. The most obvious one is professional theater, which includes Broadway, off Broadway, national road shows, and regional theaters in dozens of cities across the country. About one in four professional dancers are self-employed and manage to get gigs in TV commercials and short theatrical presentations for conventions and industrial shows. In addition, a fortunate few are hired to dance in musical numbers staged for movies and television productions.

Working Conditions

In most cases theatrical dancers split their working hours between dance studios and rehearsal halls in the daytime and actual performances onstage in the evening. The work is physically demanding, and dancers must stay in top condition at all times. The job also often requires a great deal of personal dedication and mental attention to detail.

Earnings

In 2018 the median hourly wage for professional non-Broadway theatrical dancers ranged from $14.25 to somewhat over $15.00 per hour. For the relatively few dancers who were fortunate enough to land jobs in Broadway productions, the pay was much higher—$1,754 per week (according to the prestigious New York Film Academy). In comparison, an off-Broadway dancer made less than a third of that amount—about $500 per week.

Opportunities for Advancement

The average theatrical dancer appears in an onstage chorus, a group of dancers who usually dance (and often sing) in unison. This is why they are generally referred to in the business as chorus girls or chorus boys. The first opportunity for advancement is to become a chorus leader and better yet a featured dancer, one who performs a routine by him- or herself (or with one or two other featured dancers). From there, advancement becomes extremely difficult and rare. Only a handful of dancers go on to become the leads and stars of an entire production, as did the great Gwen Verdon (1925–2000); similarly, just a few professional dancers go on to become famous choreographers, like the super talented Bob Fosse (1927–1987).

What Is the Future Outlook for Theatrical Dancers?

The call for theatrical dancers has been growing in recent years and is expected to continue to expand in the 2020s. However, according to the Bureau of Labor Statistics, job growth will be slower than average when compared to other nontheatrical professions. This is mainly because the number of young people who are training to become dancers is also rising and is expected to exceed the number of job openings in the coming years. Professional dancers will therefore continue to face very intense competition. Still, that will not stop many of those young dancers from trying. Victoria Dombroski recalls the late, legendary dancer-choreographer Merce Cunningham, saying, "You have to love dancing to stick to it. It gives you nothing back, no manuscripts to store away, no paintings to show on walls and maybe hang in museums, no poems to be printed and sold, nothing but that single fleeting moment when you feel alive."

Find Out More

American Dance Guild
320 W. Eighty-Third St., Apt. 7D
New York, NY 10024
email: adgfest@gmail.com
website: http://americandanceguild.org

The American Dance Guild is an organization that supports dancers and other artists and brings the dance community together. Each year it holds an annual festival in New York City in which it celebrates work by thirty to forty choreographers from around the world. Also, the guild's website sometimes lists upcoming auditions for dancers.

Dance USA
1029 Vermont Ave. NW, Suite 400
Washington, DC 20005
website: www.danceusa.org

Dance USA is dedicated to creating an inclusive and fair professional dance field by bringing together and supporting individual dancers, choreographers, producers, and dance companies wherever and whenever possible. Its website provides a search engine to help dancers find upcoming auditions.

National Dance Education Organization (NDEO)
8609 Second Ave., Suite 203B
Silver Spring, MD 20910
website: www.ndeo.org

The NDEO advocates using dance to help describe the human experience. The organization's website provides an events calendar for dance performances, information about upcoming conferences of members, and a useful list of dance schools and instructors.

Theatrical Costume Designer

What Does a Theatrical Costume Designer Do?

Costume designers work in film and television productions as well as in the theater. But only on occasion do such designers work in both mediums on a regular basis. Theatrical costume designers oversee the design and acquisition of costumes for stage shows. Duties are both creative and administrative; the designer fashions, or supervises the fashioning of, items having artistic quality, as well as manages the budget allotted for costumes by the theatrical producer or theater owner. Furthermore, the definition of "costumes" in the theater is frequently broad. In addition to standard clothes items, a stage costume often includes various accessories the actors wear while performing; for example, jewelry, hats, gloves, shoes, canes, crowns, hair ribbons, war medals, gun holsters, tool belts, and masks.

Depending on the wardrobe budget of the theater where the designer works, some costumes may be bought or rented from professional costume

At a Glance

Theatrical Costume Designer

Minimum Educational Requirements
An associate's degree in fashion design is recommended but not required

Personal Qualities
A high degree of creativity, willingness to work hard, good research skills, strong attention to detail

Working Conditions
Long hours in theater workrooms, rehearsal halls, and design studios

Salary Range
From $25,000 to $65,000 in 2016

Future Job Outlook
Growth of 3 percent through 2024

houses, whereas others may be made from scratch. When new costumes do need to be created, the costume designer does detailed sketches of each outfit, chooses and purchases the appropriate fabrics and other materials, and oversees the transformation of those materials into finished costumes.

The costume designer for a professional theater production normally works closely with the director and the set and lighting designers. That approach is intended to ensure that the costumes are smoothly incorporated into the production's overall look and visual themes. An obvious example would be for the costume designer and set decorator to collaborate so that the colors of the costumes and settings complement each other rather than clash.

The bigger the production and number of characters to outfit, the more help the costume designer will need. In smaller productions he or she may have only one or two assistants; in larger-scale productions—such as Broadway musicals, operas, and ballets, which tend to feature many onstage extras—the costume designer may have as many as a dozen or more assistants.

In addition to helping the costume designer make or otherwise acquire the costumes, some of those so-called wardrobe technicians, or wardrobe assistants, attend all performances. They not only help the lead actors into their initial costumes but also aid various performers in complex and/or rapid costume changes. The costume designer organizes and oversees these activities. He or she is also tasked with ensuring that the costumes in long-running productions are periodically cleaned. Indeed, the cost of dry cleaning alone can significantly increase the costume budget of a successful stage show that runs for months or longer.

How Do You Become a Theatrical Costume Designer?

Education

Most theatrical costume designers get their start in college theater productions or regional theaters and, when possible, aim to eventually find work in Broadway and/or off-Broadway productions.

A costume designer works on sketches for an upcoming theatrical production. Once the sketches are approved, the designer will choose and buy fabrics and other needed materials and oversee the transformation into finished costumes.

Some other theatrical costume designers have backgrounds in fashion design or other areas of the arts. No post–high school education is required to become a costume designer. But obtaining a college degree in theater or fashion design frequently gives a candidate an advantage over would-be designers who have no formal schooling in those areas.

In part this is because the candidates who do attend such schools gain a certain amount of hands-on experience while working in school stage productions. Also, those with such experience usually can more easily assemble an impressive portfolio of sketches and photos of their work to show to prospective employers. The latter often look for candidates who have such professional-looking portfolios. Among the more respected schools that have costume and/or fashion design programs are the New School in New York City; the Art Institute of Chicago; Baylor University in Waco, Texas; and the California College of the Arts.

Volunteer Work and Internships

A fair number of apprenticeships and internships in costume design are available for beginners in that field, often in connection with college theater departments or regional or summer theaters. Typical is the Williamstown Theatre Festival, in Williamstown, Massachusetts, which employs two to four unpaid costume interns per season. The interns work directly with the professionals in the festival's costume department. In this way the interns learn crucial costume-making skills and observe close-up the daily operations of a first-rate theatrical costume shop.

Skills and Personality

Successful theatrical costume designers always acquire a wide range of skills and abilities, chief among them creativity, which is essential to the job. Such individuals must be able to visualize in their mind's eye detailed images of people wearing costumes that do not yet exist. Moreover, the imagined outfits must be artistically appealing and appropriate for the stage or screen production they will be used in.

More tactile abilities a theatrical costume designer needs include superior drawing and sketching skills, adeptness in outlining and cutting patterns in fabric, excellent manual dexterity, diverse sewing skills, and complete familiarity with the latest computer fashion design software. A particularly important and valuable talent that all the leading costume designers possess is strong research skills, which both ensure historical accuracy and provide the designer with creative ideas. Theatrical costume designer Lynn Pecktal, a veteran of several opera and musical productions, remarks in an online interview with costume designer Dunya Ramicova, "I always do a lot of research even if the costumes I create may seem to have little to do with what I researched. Research serves as an inspiration and as a foundation to everything I do."

Costume designer Becky Bodurtha, who has taught the craft at Fordham University, agrees that doing in-depth research is vital. In an article in the career-oriented blog *Accepted*, she explains that research allows the designer to find clues to the characters' "personal history, their family history, where they live, [and] who they have relationships with, [all of which] are useful to discovering the character. I have a very long list of questions I ask; age, socio-economic status, time period, geographical location, housing, etc. That's always a great place to start, but also pretty immediately I move into image research."

Up until the late twentieth century, most of that image research was done in libraries. Although some of it still is, today far more is accomplished online. According to Canadian costume designer Judith Bowden in an interview for the online site the Secret Life of Costumes, "In the design process I think the most obvious change as a result of technology is the ability to research on the Internet. I can access museum sites with photographs of actual historical garments and vast collections. I can also go to websites of second-hand bookstores that sell primary research materials like old magazines and cutting and tailoring books."

In the personality department, an effective theatrical costume designer needs to be ambitious, driven, and willing to work long hours. He or she must also be detail oriented.

On the Job

Employers

Theatrical costume designers work in virtually all theater venues. The best-known designers work on shows that play on and off Broadway in New York City and in London's theater district, but road shows, summer stock companies, opera and ballet companies, and professional regional theaters also utilize them. In addition, hundreds of costumers and wardrobe assistants work in unpaid positions in college drama departments and the numerous community theater productions presented each year in every US state.

Working Conditions

Whether working for no pay in a community theater setting or for a competitive salary in a Broadway show, a costume designer and his or her assistants typically work long hours in jobs that can be very demanding. Moreover, the designer is expected to wear many hats and to accomplish a wide variety of duties. First, he or she reads the play that will be staged and takes extensive notes on the characters and their backgrounds and personalities. The designer then meets with other key people working on the production. In fact, production meetings are frequent during the weeks (and on occasion, months) during which a production is being mounted. This is essential for the coordination and teamwork necessary for the play to become a success. In Bowden's words:

> I work in collaboration with a number of people, but first with the director. I assist in the collaborative process by presenting [him or her] with visual references, sketches, collages etc., in order to make sure that the images and ideas that I describe are on par with what [he or she] envisions as we continue to meet and discuss. . . . Theater is an intensely collaborative art form, and it's essential to learn how to work as a team.

In between meetings, the costume designer oversees the making and/or buying of the costumes. The work takes place in varied settings. These can include the costume department or workroom of a theater, rehearsal halls (where meetings with the director and actors might happen), or the designer's own home or design studio. The designer also travels regularly to buy fabric and other materials or to inspect the inventory at costume houses.

Earnings

The salary of a theatrical costume designer will vary somewhat, depending on his or her experience and reputation. Designers who are just starting out in the business can expect to make somewhere between $25,000 and $35,000 annually. If they have experience, earning $40,000 to $45,000 annually is possible. A handful of the best-known designers may earn up to $65,000 or more yearly.

Opportunities for Advancement

For theatrical costume designers who work in community theater, regional theater, or other relatively small or isolated venues, making it to off Broadway and particularly Broadway itself is a common goal for advancement within the theater world. A few of the most successful theatrical costume designers make the leap into designing costumes for feature films, where a designer can make thousands of dollars per day and have his or her work seen by hundreds of millions of people worldwide. But successfully making that leap is a rare occurrence in the entertainment industry.

What Is the Future Outlook for Theatrical Costume Designers?

The occupation of theatrical costume designer is highly specialized; also, only a few thousand job openings exist each year in the profession, which means that competition for those jobs tends to be fierce. As a result, growth in the number of openings for new theatrical costume designers is expected to remain either stagnant or slow in the near future. Experts predict a growth rate of only 3 percent or less through at least 2024. Nevertheless, as the Bureau of Labor Statistics points out, the minority of designers who have both a lot of experience and impressive portfolios will almost always be considered first for those few new job opportunities that do arise.

Find Out More

Costume Designers Guild (CDG)
3919 W. Magnolia Blvd.
Burbank, CA 91505
website: https://costumedesignersguild.com

The CDG is dedicated to raising the stature of the costume designer profession in the entertainment industry. The organization and its website provide helpful information about upcoming costume-related public events, important news about the costume industry, and a useful archive of articles about specific costume designers and their achievements.

Costume Society of America (CSA)
PO Box 852
Columbus, GA 31902
website: http://costumesocietyamerica.com

The CSA works to bring about an understanding of dress and fashion practices of people around the world, using research, education, preservation, and design. The website provides members and would-be designers with information about upcoming meetings of designers, as well as a community forum in which anyone can raise and discuss ideas and issues.

National Costumers Association (NCA)
2851 S. Parker Rd., Suite 1210
Aurora, CO 80014
website: https://www.costumers.org

The NCA is a professional group that promotes the artistic, educational, social, and historical nature of costuming. Its website allows members and others to subscribe to *Costumer* magazine and contains a fulsome section for students, including how to obtain scholarships to design school and how to enter a design competition open to students.

Theatrical Lighting Designer

What Does a Theatrical Lighting Designer Do?

Lighting designers who work in theater and other live entertainment venues utilize the powerful and highly creative medium of light to fashion visual effects that enhance the setting and mood of the story and onstage action. Of course, without lights, the audience would not be able to see the actors and sets. Yet beyond that basic function of theatrical lighting are all sorts of imaginative and often beautiful uses.

One of the simplest but most effective is to indicate the time of day that the story, or parts of it, takes place. Other, more complex uses of light include matching the color scheme of the sets and costumes; dividing the stage into separate pools of light, each representing a different time and place; and creating bold, even startling dramatic effects, including rendering the actors in silhouette. In the words of successful theatrical lighting designer Patrick Woodroffe in an interview for the website

At a Glance

Theatrical Lighting Designer

Minimum Educational Requirements
None

Personal Qualities
Artistic, creative flair; perfect color vision; willingness to work hard; ability to collaborate with others

Working Conditions
Long hours spent hanging lights in theaters, stadiums, and other venues; working around electricity; in some cases traveling with touring companies

Salary Range
From $40,000 to $70,000 annually in 2019, although a handful of top designers can make more

Future Job Outlook
Growth of 7 percent through 2024

Job Shadow, "With the technology that exists nowadays lighting is often used as a piece of scenery in its own right, particularly in large scale events such as stadium rock shows, for example, where the lighting is a show in itself—a light show if you like. Lighting is an important tool in shaping a performance and the role of the lighting designer is key to the success of a live event."

In addition to planning the lighting effects themselves, lighting designers have numerous other important duties and functions. They hire a crew of assistants, for example, assign them various tasks, and oversee them as a unit within the overall production crew. Lighting designers also manage the budget allotted by the producer or theater manager for the show's lighting.

Working with the assistants, these designers also maintain a detailed and accurate inventory of all lights, dimmers, colored gels, electrical cables, and so forth. They create a program— today often computerized—of all lighting changes and either run or train someone to run the program during performances. In addition, lighting designers work closely with the director, set decorator, and costume designer to make sure the show has an overall coordinated look or theme.

How Do You Become a Theatrical Lighting Designer?

Education

Theatrical lighting designers usually take one of two general educational or training paths. A few lucky individuals might manage to land an entry-level job on a lighting crew for a theater, ballet company, rock band, road show of a play, or other entertainment venue that requires professional lighting. These individuals learn the ropes on the job a little at a time and hopefully are able to advance through the ranks to positions of more responsibility and authority. This is how Woodroffe got his start; he later became one of the most respected lighting designers in the world. "I started at the bottom of the ladder," he recalls, and "happened to be at the right place at the right time."

The more common way that theatrical lighting designers learn their craft is by attending colleges or other schools that offer programs in lighting design. The most coveted degree is called a master of fine arts in lighting design. Several dozen American colleges and technical schools offer this degree or close equivalents. Among the institutions with excellent reputations are Colorado State University in Fort Collins, the University of Michigan in Ann Arbor, the American Academy of Dramatic Arts in Los Angeles, the New England Conservatory in Boston, and the University of Virginia in Charlottesville.

Volunteer Work and Internships

Various colleges and technical schools that have programs in theater-related arts offer internships in lighting design, as do regional and summer theaters. The Weston Playhouse Theatre Company in Weston, Vermont, is a good example. The company hired two lighting interns for the 2019 season. The interns worked alongside the professional lighting technicians, costumers, and actors, affording the initiates the chance to observe the intricacies of play production, including lighting, firsthand. Young people interested in theatrical lighting internships should check the websites of various college and professional theaters.

Skills and Personality

Theatrical lighting designers need to display a number of skills, some of them artistic and creative, others technical and administrative. First they must be able to visualize complex lighting setups and schemes in their mind's eye and then translate such visions into reality using lights of different colors. In fact, because color is so often involved in the work, it is essential that a lighting designer have perfect color vision. (There is no way to fake having this skill, since the inability to recognize all colors will make it impossible for someone to create a credible lighting program.)

On the administrative side, successful lighting designers must be able to manage a team of technicians and make, keep track of, and update the lighting budget. From a technical standpoint, superior knowledge of the different kinds of theatrical lights is required, as is knowledge of electrical wiring, consoles, circuits, and projection equipment. Designers must also have a working knowledge of the latest computer software available for various forms of entertainment lighting.

Designers should possess a personality that allows them to easily deal with certain professional and social situations. They have to communicate effectively with directors, stage managers, and actors on a regular basis and must be flexible, detail oriented, resourceful, and able to handle multiple tasks at the same time. Finally, designers need to understand that the job requires working long, often irregular hours, evening hours, and sometimes weekends.

On the Job

Employers

In addition to plays staged in theaters, lighting designers are hired to light many other kinds of entertainment venues. Woodroffe supplies this informative overview of the most typical ones:

> I create the lighting for a variety of different events, but mostly ones involving actors or performers. These include live concerts by everyone from rock-and-roll bands to classical artists . . . classical and contemporary operas, ballet and various forms of dance, musical theater and arena spectacles and various special events. I also light more esoteric odd things like fashion shows, special parties. . . . I also create architectural schemes where the lighting is deliberately theatrical, [for example] for a Las Vegas hotel or nightclub, or a lighting design for a public space where the drama of the lighting enhances the experience at night.

As Woodroffe's list of venues demonstrates, theatrical lighting designers can provide creative lighting arrangements for a surprisingly wide array of live public presentations.

Working Conditions

Typically, theatrical lighting designers first read the script, if working on a play, or study the events, music, or other elements presented in other entertainment venues that must be lit. Then they inspect the theater stage, stadium, auditorium, or other physical space where the action to be lit will take place. Next they visualize a lighting scheme and present a detailed description of it to the director. Meetings follow, along with overseeing the acquisition and placement of the lights. It is also common for the designer to attend at least some rehearsals to get a feel for the lighting cues that will match up with various lines spoken by the actors.

The lighting designer also spends a fair amount of the time traveling to appropriate commercial outlets to rent or buy equipment. For the busy designers who do the lighting for pop and rock musicians on the road, traveling is frequently more extensive. Woodroffe points out,

> I spend a lot of time traveling, working on different productions all over the world, perhaps twenty projects each year. So I could literally be having breakfast at my kitchen table at home in England, eating lunch in a diner on the East Coast of America, or having a drink in a bar in Singapore. This is one of the great attractions of the job and what makes it so unusually rewarding.

Earnings

The pay for theatrical lighting designers tends to vary according to the specific venue and designer. Most individuals in the business, who work in theaters that present plays, ballets, operas, and so forth, made an average of $58,000 in 2019. (The location of the theater, its financial resources, and the designer's level of experience were factors that dictated whether he or she made less or more than that average.) A handful of lighting designers who have major names in the business and who handle the light shows for the touring shows of world-class entertainers or bands—an elite group that includes Woodroffe—may earn as much as $250,000 or more annually.

Opportunities for Advancement

In general, lighting designers who work in Broadway and off-Broadway theaters make more per show than those who work in regional theaters and summer stock. Also, working in shows presented in New York City or London significantly enhances a designer's reputation. Thus, one avenue for advancement within the business is to compete for jobs in those cities.

Another way to advance in the profession is to land positions in the touring companies of major entertainers, including pop singers like Beyoncé, Justin Timberlake, and Lady Gaga and classic rock bands like the Rolling Stones and Journey. The light shows for their concerts are usually extremely large scale and widely reviewed, and the producers pay the lighting designers top dollar.

What Is the Future Outlook for Theatrical Lighting Designers?

Both the Bureau of Labor Statistics and experts within the entertainment industry predict a moderate growth rate of 7 percent for theatrical lighting designers through 2024. Thus, at least a few thousand paying jobs will be available in this specialized field.

With few jobs, competition is fierce. Unfortunately, the struggle for jobs is also impacted by gender bias. Traditionally, most theatrical lighting design jobs have gone to men, even when qualified women were available. A survey conducted for the League of Resident Theatres examined seasons spanning the period from 2012 to 2016 and found that three-quarters of all the new lighting design jobs went to men. Similarly, from May 2010 to April 2017, most of the lighting designers in the twenty-three off-Broadway theaters in New York City were held by men. "It's pretty scary, the statistics," remarks Kathy Perkins in an article for the website American Theatre. One of the few successful female lighting designers, she says, "It's gotten a little better, but it's still pretty bad," and adds, "in my generation, there have been women who just completely left the field because they couldn't find work." Perkins and other concerned women in the business continue to urge theater producers and managers to be more equitable in hiring lighting designers, but the future for women in the field remains unclear.

Find Out More

International Alliance of Theatrical Stage Employees (IATSE)
207 W. Twenty-Fifth St., Fourth Floor
New York, NY 10001
website: www.iatse.net

The IATSE's members work for theaters, trade shows, concerts, and the construction shops that make technical equipment for these venues, including lighting equipment. The group's website provides information about scholarships, training programs for young people, and health benefits for members and their families.

International Association of Lighting Designers (IALD)
440 N. Wells St., Suite 210
Chicago, IL 60654
website: www.iald.org

The IALD promotes the advancement and recognition of professional lighting designers. The organization's website provides information about upcoming meetings of lighting designers, describes a student training program called Learn2Light, and lists a number of current job opportunities for its members.

United States Institute for Theatre Technology (USITT)
290 Elwood Davis Rd., Suite 100
Liverpool, NY 13088
website: www.usitt.org

The USITT was founded in 1960 to promote dialogue, research, and learning among practitioners of theater design and technology, including lighting design. The USITT website lists various job openings and provides a good deal of information about schools, classes, and other training for professionals in the technical sectors of theater production.

Film and TV Makeup Artist

What Does a Film and TV Makeup Artist Do?

Makeup artists who work on the sets of movies and television shows help actors undergo visual transformations into the characters the actors portray in those productions. As an actor does to him- or herself in a stage play, a makeup artist makes the actor look more beautiful, uglier, older, younger, or whatever look for that character is called for in the script. Indeed, the successful makeup expert is adept at several different approaches to makeup. One is the application of standard beauty makeup to accentuate an actor's eyes, lips, hairstyle, and other features. Another is doing age makeups on younger actors whose characters grow older during the story.

Still another approach that makeup artists employ is to create complex specialty makeups, well-known examples of which include characters with deformities; diseases; bruises, cuts, and other injuries; scars, and so forth. This category also typically includes imaginary, fanciful, or monstrous

At a Glance

Film and TV Makeup Artist

Minimum Educational Requirements
None

Personal Qualities
Creativity, artistic abilities, manual dexterity, attention to detail

Working Conditions
On busy sets or alone doing preparatory work, often at home

Salary Range
About $37,000 to $75,000 in 2017

Number of Jobs
About 3,000 in 2017

Future Job Outlook
Growth of up to 19 percent through 2024

characters, such as the Mad Hatter in *Alice in Wonderland* and Quasimodo the bell ringer in *The Hunchback of Notre Dame*, along with witches, vampires, werewolves, and all manner of alien beings. Most often these more extreme types of makeup require the makeup master to fashion prosthetics: rubber or foam noses, chins, cheeks, ears, and other pieces specifically made to perfectly fit an actor's face and head. Beards, mustaches, and wigs, as well as false teeth and body makeup, are also common in such visual transformations.

If only one or two characters in a film or TV show require extensive makeup, a makeup artist may work with the aid of a single assistant. Much more often, however, a large number of characters must be made up, in which case the chief makeup artist may command a crew of a dozen or more assistants, including hairstylists and sometimes wig makers. Very large-scale movies can employ small armies of makeup people. Each of Peter Jackson's three epic *Lord of the Rings* films utilized more than fifty makeup artists and required hundreds of handmade wigs.

Well-known makeup artist Greg Nicotero, makeup supervisor for the hit AMC TV series *The Walking Dead*, continually works with a similar crew of assistants. To accomplish realistic "rotting" effects for many dozens of actors playing zombies in each episode, Nicotero learned to use his crew to save time and money. In an online article about the making of the show, he explains,

> We have an assembly line of four artists that can finish 40 to 50 zombies in an hour. The first makeup artist shadows around the eyes and cheekbones, the next person does a lighter color over the highlights to accentuate the bone structure, the next person spatters blood, and then the last person puts conditioner in their hair.

A makeup artist's job may not end with the preparation and application of makeup. In some cases he or she stays on the set for much of a shooting day to do touch-ups to the makeup of principal players. In addition, if a makeup is very complex and cumbersome, the makeup artist or one of his or her assistants will help the actor remove the makeup at the end of the day.

How Do You Become a Film and TV Makeup Artist?

Education

No specific academic schooling or other formal training is required for someone to become a film and television makeup artist. In fact, most makeup artists start out as self-taught lovers of movies and movie makeup who manage to land jobs as unpaid makeup interns or assistants on small TV or movie sets. Over time, they compile portfolios (collections of photos and credits) that they show to better-known makeup artists or film and TV producers.

This was the route taken by the late Dick Smith (1922–2014), widely viewed as the world's leading makeup artist for several decades. "For me," he said in an interview with a young, aspiring makeup artist in 1967,

> it all started when I came across a quaint little book titled *Paint, Paste and Makeup*. After reading it and doing some experimental makeups, I volunteered to do the makeup for actors in the small productions they put on at the Yale drama department. A few years later I showed my portfolio to some TV people and NBC hired me to be in charge of [their] makeup department.

In recent years, many young makeup artists have instead chosen the academic route by taking makeup courses in private drama schools or colleges with large theater departments. Though workable, that approach has not proved any more beneficial than the self-taught one. This is because sooner or later a beginning makeup artist, regardless of his or her initial approach, must show a portfolio to movie or TV producers and hope for the best.

33

Volunteer Work and Internships

Aspiring makeup artists can still volunteer to ply their craft in school shows, as Smith did, or in community theater productions. This provides valuable practice and opportunity to experiment with makeup techniques without being judged harshly by professional experts. Internships, especially paid ones, are few and hard to get; those legitimate ones that exist usually consist of assisting an established makeup artist as a sort of apprentice for a certain length of time.

In contrast, ads for so-called makeup interns—to work unpaid on low-budget films in exchange for a screen credit—are more often than not designed to exploit young makeup artists' talents without having to pay them. Each artist should investigate the producer's and director's background and carefully decide whether the time and effort will be worth it. A few such gigs do lead to more and better makeup jobs, but most do not.

Skills and Personality

Makeup artists must be creative and, as the name of the occupation indicates, artistically inclined. In fact, all makeup artists possess the innate ability to draw human faces with at least a fair degree of competence, and some are gifted sketch artists or painters. This talent comes in handy in planning makeups, especially complex, involved ones. Makeup artists should also have good manual dexterity and a keen eye for detail.

Those inborn abilities aside, successful makeup artists need to develop a set of solid skills, all of which improve with practice and frequent repetition. They should become adept not only at doing standard beauty and glamour makeup but also at applying false beards and mustaches; aging a young face through paint (brushed-on makeup) alone; and doing the same in three dimensions with prosthetics. Properly done, the latter should look completely real even to someone standing a few feet away.

Creating the plaster "life masks" needed to make such realistic prosthetics is another skill a professional makeup artist must master, as well as the ability to sculpt the individual prosthetics in

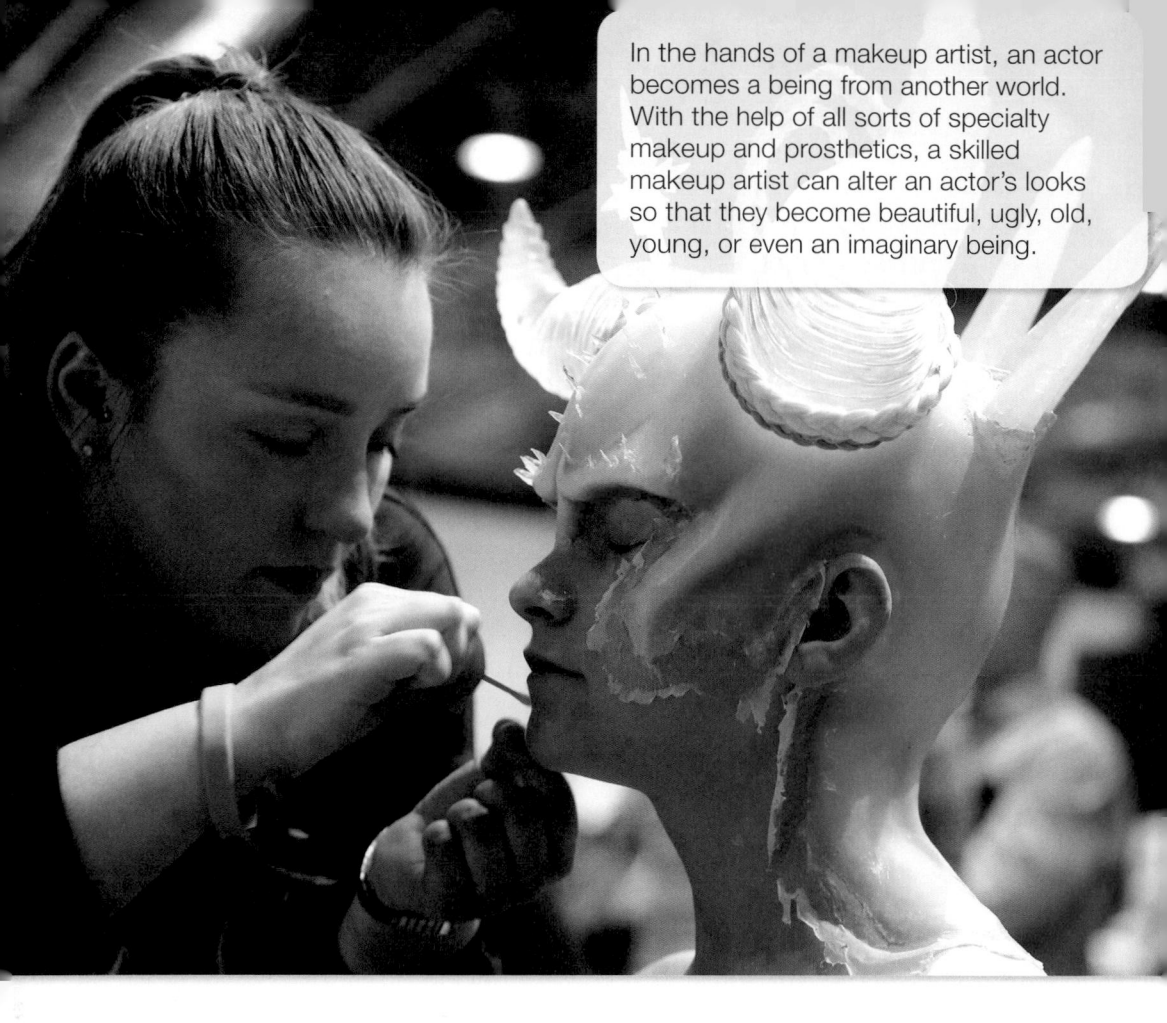

In the hands of a makeup artist, an actor becomes a being from another world. With the help of all sorts of specialty makeup and prosthetics, a skilled makeup artist can alter an actor's looks so that they become beautiful, ugly, old, young, or even an imaginary being.

clay before transforming them into rubber or foam. Other necessary skills include applying bald caps, wigs, hairpieces, and body makeup and creating all sorts of special applications, including scars, injuries, false teeth and eyes, and various monster effects.

In addition, makeup artists should be familiar with the principal brands of stage and film makeup and know how to order their products when needed. They should also learn to work within a set budget and be well organized and prepared when actors arrive early in the morning to have their makeup applied. Successful makeup artists should be skilled as well at doing research on historical trends in beard, mustache, and hairstyles over the centuries. Finally, they should be familiar with the work and books of the great makeup artists of the past, including Lon Chaney, Dick Smith, Rick Baker, and Stan Winston.

Employers

Film and TV makeup artists are typically needed for feature films, experimental films, student films, filmed or videotaped television shows, music videos, and TV commercials. Live television shows also sometimes employ them, as do awards shows like the Oscars, Emmys, and Tonys. Meanwhile, one of the Oscars is handed out annually to the best achievement in makeup.

Working Conditions

Like so many other people who work on films and television shows, makeup artists tend to put in long workdays; twelve to fourteen hours or more per day is not unusual. This can have financial benefits because if the artist works longer than a set number of hours—in many industry contracts ten—he or she receives overtime pay.

Makeup artists' hours are also often irregular and erratic. They do spend many hours in dressing rooms on film and TV sets, applying or touching up actors' makeups. In addition, when they are not working on actors on a set, makeup artists frequently spend time at odd hours of the day or night making prosthetic pieces and wigs or devising or preparing various special makeup effects. This also means that sometimes makeup artists work closely with large numbers of people and other times may spend many hours by themselves doing research and testing makeup. In an interview for the blog *Unknown Beauty*, noted special effects wizard Thomas Surprenant, who did the makeup for the television series *Buffy the Vampire Slayer*, says he always conducts research on makeup materials and does "many test makeups before actual shooting begins." He adds, "I think research is extremely important, not just for a look for a character, but also for materials that will look the best."

Earnings

The earnings of film and TV makeup artists vary widely, based partly on their experience and reputation and also on the details of individual contracts made with the producers of the movies and television shows in question. According to the *Hollywood Reporter*, in 2017–2018 the salary range for makeup artists in the industry was roughly $37,000 to $75,000 per year. However, the more famous and in-demand makeup artists—makeup superstars such as Baker and Winston, for instance—can make up to $125,000 or considerably more annually.

Opportunities for Advancement

Makeup artists advance in their careers almost totally as a result of their talent, skills, experience, and reputation. A person is either the head makeup artist on a production or one of his or her assistants. So an assistant can aspire to be the head of the makeup unit, but beyond that an enhanced reputation and the clout to make more money per production are the chief forms of advancement.

What Is the Future Outlook for Film and TV Makeup Artists?

During the 2020s the occupation of film and TV makeup artist is expected to remain viable and expand. The Bureau of Labor Statistics predicts a growth rate for makeup artist jobs of up to 19 percent through 2024. This will largely be due to the continuing popularity of big-budget science fiction, fantasy, horror, and superhero movies and TV shows, all of which call for numerous character, creature, and monster makeups.

Find Out More

Academy of Television Arts and Sciences
5220 Lankershim Blvd.
North Hollywood, CA 91601
website: www.emmys.com

The Academy of Television Arts and Sciences, which presents the yearly Emmys broadcast, is devoted to the advancement of television sciences and artistic endeavors, including the makeup arts. Its website contains helpful articles about the TV business; it also offers much data on internship programs and how to apply, plus interviews with current interns.

International Makeup Artists Trade Show (IMATS)
12808 NE Ninety-Fifth St.
Vancouver, WA 98682
website: https://imats.net

IMATS holds four to five large-scale trade shows each year in different cities. Both professional and aspiring makeup artists gather to show off their talents. The organization and its website promote constant training for makeup artists everywhere. The website tells how to obtain tickets for the shows.

Make-Up Artists & Hair Stylists Guild
http://www.local706.org

The Make-Up Artists & Hair Stylists Guild is the official labor union for film makeup artists and hairstylists. Its website keeps members and visitors up-to-date on the latest news about the film makeup business. The website also helps visitors obtain issues of the union's magazine, the *Artisan*, which contains information about makeup techniques and current job openings.

Film and TV Composer

What Does a Film and TV Composer Do?

Film and TV composers create musical scores for motion pictures, television shows, or other entertainment venues. For that reason, they are sometimes called scorers. One of the greatest scorers of the golden age of film music (the 1930s through the 1960s), Alfred Newman, once described his job as "sitting in a room, wearing out pencils." His comment appears on the American Composers Orchestra website.

Newman's joke aside, today's leading film composers—including Newman's sons David Newman (*Night School*) and Thomas Newman (*Bridge of Spies*), as well as noted scorer Hans Zimmer (*The Dark Knight*)—fully recognize that their job is to use music to enhance the dramatic and visual qualities of a film. These expert composers realize that they can make a sad scene even sadder, as well as help the audience better understand an on-screen character's personality and emotions. Indeed, on many different levels, a thoughtful score can heighten viewers' appreciation for a movie or TV show and at times add distinction and artistic quality to an otherwise average production.

At a Glance

Film and TV Composer

Minimum Educational Requirements
None

Personal Qualities
Strong artistic tendencies, ability to hear new music in one's head, wide knowledge of music history and styles, love of movies and film scores

Working Conditions
Mostly solitary work composing music at home, most often on a computer

Salary Range
From $15,000 to $100,000 in 2018

Number of Jobs
About 7,000 to 8,000 in 2018

Future Job Outlook
Growth of 6 percent through 2026

Furthermore, scorers are also in a very real sense music teachers who instill either a love or appreciation for good music in audience members, even though the latter rarely realize this is happening. In a book about his Oscar-winning score to the 1959 epic *Ben-Hur*, another composer of the golden age, Miklós Rózsa, remarked that film music reaches an enormous audience. "Its educational value is greater than that of concerts, radio, or records. [Thus] the film composer bears the responsibility for forming the musical taste of a new generation."

Scorers generally work during the last phase of making a movie or TV show—called postproduction—after most or all the principal photography is completed. Having viewed the edited or semiedited footage, they compose an appropriate score. If many instruments are involved, which is often the case, these composers will either orchestrate the music themselves or hand it over to a professional orchestrator.

How Do You Become a Film and TV Composer?

Education

A film and TV composer does not require any special training or education. In fact, some composers are self-taught and learn by doing. Nevertheless, several of the more successful American film composers attended four-year college music programs. Some of the better-known US colleges that offer music scoring programs are Berklee College of Music in Boston, Manhattan School of Music in New York City, and the University of California, Los Angeles. Ultimately, says Robert Allaire, veteran scorer for a number of TV series, it does not matter which of these approaches a beginning scorer takes. On the website Careers in Film, he points out, "A rich background in music is key. For some that might mean formal training at a university or conservatory, while others with a different background might be inclined to dive right in."

Regardless of which initial educational path the fledgling composer takes, finding work as a film and TV scorer is extremely difficult. This is because there are relatively few scoring jobs to be had at any given time; yet there are always a great many would-be composers competing for those jobs. Therefore, breaking into scoring is not just about talent. Much of it has to do with being in the right place at the right time. In an incident well known in the industry (and reported on the website Chron), the famous modern scorer John Williams (*Jaws*, *E.T.*, *Star Wars*) was approached by a newcomer, who asked, "What will it take to become a film composer?" Williams smiled and responded, "Well, the first thing is, you need a few good breaks." After a pause, he added, "About thirty of them."

Volunteer Work and Internships

Young, inexperienced composers can and do volunteer to compose music for student films and other amateur productions, positions that are almost always unpaid. Such gigs may or may not lead the composer into a professional career but do tend to be good practice because they offer some hands-on experience.

Meanwhile, several film and music companies and producers offer internships in various aspects of film and TV music. Again, these can provide a person some valuable beginner's experience. But most such positions involve little or no actual music scoring. The reality is summed up well by a disclaimer on the website of London music producer Jim Hustwit, who does take on a few music interns each year: "We want to be completely honest and it is important to understand that when you start out you will not be scoring films and producing top 10 artists. As an intern you will start with very basic tasks which may be more related to the running of the studio." Such honesty may deter some aspiring composers, but most recognize that any opportunity to work within the field is not to be dismissed.

Skills and Personality

Successful film and TV scorers must be masters of many skills, some of them artistic and others mechanical or technical. On the artistic side, they must be highly creative. It is essential that these individuals be able to "hear" new music in their heads, preferably at least some of it in finished, orchestrated form. Scorers must also know how to notate (write down) that imagined music for all standard instruments. Although they do not have to be able to play any instruments, the ability to sound out chords on a keyboard is extremely helpful. They must also be highly conversant with music history and its various periods and composing styles.

On the technical side, scorers must be skilled at using one or more of the computerized notation programs now seen as standard in the business, the best known being Sibelius. These programs allow scorers to enter music on a computer monitor and hear playback of partial or finished scores supplied by digitalized instrument sounds. Knowledge of how to operate professional recording equipment is also helpful.

Finally, composers must be able to adapt to artistic changes and the new demands that frequently materialize while the score is being created and never take themselves too seriously. On his popular Twitter feed, the talented Hans Zimmer stated, "You have to remain flexible and you must be your own critic at all times."

On the Job

Employers
All film and television studios employ musical scorers. Some maintain close connections with specific talented scorers and use them repeatedly for studio productions. Many of the most well-known scorers work independently and are hired by studios when a director or the producers believe a film or TV show would benefit from the skills of a certain scorer. In addition to composing music for feature films and TV shows, scorers sometimes get hired for jobs of smaller scope, including providing music for TV commercials and video games.

Working Conditions
Although music scorers work mainly in the postproduction phase of film and television, they sometimes provide the director with some basic themes or other snippets even during preproduction

(the phase before principal photography begins). This can aid the director in better visualizing the emotional feel of the drama. During postproduction the job of music composition is fast paced and demanding. "It's not unusual for me to work sixteen-hour days, seven days a week," Allaire says.

Usually, the scorer spends most of his or her time alone at home, entering the music into Sibelius or whichever computerized notation program he or she owns. However, phone calls or visits to the director are common. Howard Shore, who scored the three epic *Lord of the Rings* films, explains in an interview for the website Collider, "I usually work with the director and it's just a collaboration between me and the one person. I think you make good movies that way. If the director and the composer can have this common goal and this excitement about making something great, then you're going to do something good."

Earnings

There is no set fee for doing a film or TV score. Earnings can vary widely, depending on the size and budget of the film or TV show, the amount of music created, and the composer's experience and reputation. A scorer might make as little as $15,000 for working on an episode of a TV show or more than $100,000 for scoring a feature film. The rough average per-project earnings for working film composers in 2017 was about $50,000. (Only a small handful of scorers do more than one project in a given year.) Fewer than ten scorers are famous enough to command the so-called big bucks, which can amount to more than $1 million a year. Among that musical elite are John Williams, Hans Zimmer, and Danny Elfman (*The Avengers: Age of Ultron*).

Opportunities for Advancement

No single path to advancement exists for film and TV composers. Those who aspire to join the profession and have not yet produced a score should network as much as they are able within the movie and television industries. If possible, they should apply to become assistants to working composers. Such positions, which are few, usually consist of running errands for the composer; if the assistant is fortunate, he or she might end up doing a bit of orchestration for the boss. Once a fledgling composer has produced one or more scores, advancement consists mainly of seeking out more work and trying to build a bigger reputation. "There isn't really one tried-and-true path for aspiring composers," Allaire says. "Every working composer will have a different story of how they got to the position they're in."

What Is the Future Outlook for Film and TV Composers?

There will always be a need for film and television scorers in feature films, TV series, and video games. However, industry analysts estimate that at most between seven thousand and eight thousand composers will work at all in a given year in the 2020s. Yet at least seventy-five thousand aspiring scorers, many of them quite talented, will compete for those few assignments. Therefore, anyone who dreams of doing this highly creative job needs to want it very badly and be willing to spend years of concerted effort trying to make that dream a reality.

Find Out More

American Society of Composers, Authors and Publishers (ASCAP)
250 W. Fifty-Seventh St.
New York, NY 10107
website: www.ascap.com

ASCAP is a professional organization of 690,000 songwriters, composers, and music publishers, owned and run by its members. Its detailed website provides information about how to make money from one's music and how to license that music to be properly paid by listeners. The website also contains revealing interviews with popular songwriters.

Independent Filmmaker Project (IFP)
30 John St., Ground Floor
Brooklyn, NY 11201
website: www.ifp.org

The IFP works with independent film artists, including composers, across the world. Its website explains how the organization helps independent artists find both funding and expert advisers. In these and other ways, the IFP aids independent filmmakers in the production of about 350 projects each year. Each project needs a composer, which affords those scorers valuable experience.

Society of Composers & Lyricists (SCL)
8306 Wilshire Blvd., Suite 512
Beverly Hills, CA 90211
website: http://thescl.com

The SCL provides a wealth of information and services for composers and musicians of all ages. Its website features a calendar of upcoming musical events, explains how young composers can find experienced composers to be their mentors, and gives information about available educational seminars in which the participants learn about scoring methods.

Film and TV Director

What Does a Film and TV Director Do?

Whether working on a feature film, a TV show, a TV commercial, a music video, or some other entertainment format, a director is the artistic boss. (In contrast, the producer is the administrative, financial boss, who raises the money for the project and hires the director and other personnel.) The director oversees the various members of the film crew and makes sure they turn his or her vision of the story into reality. As Jared Januschka, director of the 2018 feature film *Shooting in Vain*, puts it in an article for the website Careers in Film, "The Director is responsible for everything that goes into a production from an artistic standpoint and is required to be well-versed in every aspect of the filmmaking process, enabling him or her to speak with each department in that discipline's own particular language. . . . It's a very fluid process that requires strong problem-solving skills."

Before shooting begins, in the preparatory phase of filmmaking called preproduction, the director meets with the

At a Glance

Film and TV Director

Minimum Educational Requirements
None

Personal Qualities
A degree of creativity, a love and fascination for films, strong attention to detail, excellent communication skills

Working Conditions
Long hours spent on busy sets at studios or in a wide variety of outside locations

Salary Range
Varies widely, from $300 to $6,000 per day

Number of Jobs
About 60,000+, including TV commercials, music videos, TV episodes, documentaries, and full-length movies

Future Job Outlook
Growth of 12 percent through 2024

heads of the various production departments—camera, sound, costumes, editing, music scoring, and so forth. He or she explains his or her personal vision and expectations for the project. The director also ensures that locations are scouted and sets are constructed, and he or she chooses the actors in collaboration with the producer.

During the production, or shooting, phase of the project, the director runs the set and guides the various production crews in a synchronized effort to complete a work. Saying "action" and "cut" and getting the various scenes recorded on film is only one facet of the job. The director also answers the numerous questions inevitably posed by crew members on a given day and views the dailies (footage shot that day) to make sure they are usable.

During postproduction, the director oversees the jobs done by the editor, music scorer, special effects crew, and others who piece together and/or enhance the footage shot in the production phase. Once the project is finally "in the can," in filmmaking lingo, it enters the distribution phase. Usually, the director, along with the producer and leading actors, helps promote the film through interviews and appearances at film premieres and festivals.

How Do You Become a Film and TV Director?

Education

No specific schooling or other training is mandatory to become a film and TV director. In 1940 twenty-five-year-old Orson Welles, who had no training as a director and had never even worked on a movie set before, directed *Citizen Kane*, widely viewed even today as one of the greatest films ever made. Although an exceptional case, it does illustrate that some people have an innate talent for directing and can do the job without extensive training.

Today would-be film directors follow varied paths to the job. Some attend four-year colleges that offer degrees in film production or film directing. Among the best-known and in-demand college film schools are those at New York University in New

York City; the University of Southern California, Los Angeles; and Emerson College in Boston.

Other prospective film directors choose a nonacademic route in which they start in small jobs on various kinds of movie or TV sets and over time steadily work their way up through the ranks. Although Januschka did attend film school, he strongly advocates the other path for those who cannot afford college. "The most important training for becoming a film director," he says, "is to watch movies and work on film sets."

Volunteer Work and Internships

Volunteer positions and internships in which a person with no experience actually gets to direct part or all of a film project do not exist. However, a fair number of unpaid internships in various aspects of film production *can* be found across the country. Film and video production companies, both small and large, offer such positions, and at least some of the interns in those programs later go on to directing careers.

Typical is the internship in film editing offered in 2019 by Interlock Media in Cambridge, Massachusetts. Although the position offered no actual directing opportunities, the intern did help a professional editor and thereby met and worked closely with a professional director during postproduction. In a similar vein, Warner Brothers Studio is one of the larger film companies that sponsors internships in filmmaking. Each year as many as twenty young aspiring filmmakers work for ten weeks in studio departments ranging from marketing and publicity to digital media and media research. In addition, a few of the interns are allowed to watch directors at work on professional sets. Learning the trade and making contacts can help open doors for aspiring directors.

Skills and Personality

One of the chief skills directors must possess is the ability to conceptualize a movie when reading the script. That is, they should be able to visualize in their mind's eye how the finished film will look. Other important skills needed for the job include knowledge of the full production process and all the various departments, meticulous attention to detail, and strong written and verbal communication skills. Indeed, says Januschka, "The better a communicator he is, the more he will know, and [the more] time will be saved."

This ability to do good, artistic work in a minimum time frame is a key part of the larger skill of completing a project on time and on budget. The renowned modern director Ridley Scott (*Aliens*, *Gladiator*) believes that this is one of a director's most crucial skills. Yet surprisingly, he points out in an interview for the trade magazine *Variety*, "Film school never teaches you that."

Above all, a director must be adept at telling a story to the audience in a memorable way. The late, esteemed director Alfred Hitchcock (*Psycho*, *The Birds*) said that this storytelling skill should rely on using a minimal number of shots, or cuts, each meaningful in its own right. In the article about filmmaking he wrote for the *Encyclopaedia Britannica*, Hitchcock said:

> In a play, the action is moved forward in words. The film director moves his action forward with a camera—whether that action is set on a prairie or confined to a telephone booth. He always must be searching for some new way of making his statement, and above all he must make it with the . . . greatest economy of cutting; that is to say, in the minimum of shots. Each shot must be as comprehensive a statement as possible, reserving cutting for dramatic purposes. The impact of the image is of the first importance in a medium that directs the concentration of the eye so that it cannot stray.

While making a statement might be the worthwhile goal of directing, the most accomplished directors recognize that bringing together the talents of an entire crew will make that objective easier to achieve.

Employers

Directors work mostly on feature films and episodic television shows for established studios. However, they are also regularly hired to do TV commercials for companies that are often connected to major studios. It is well known in the industry, for instance, that Ridley Scott directed close to three thousand commercials before getting the opportunity to direct his first feature film. Directors also do music videos, documentaries, and other short subjects; animated films; and video games.

Working Conditions

Directors, particularly those making large-scale projects like feature films, tend to have tight, demanding schedules. They are usually constantly busy, whether it be with rewriting the script with the screenwriter, shooting scenes, meeting with the producer and/or department heads, rehearsing actors, or solving problems that inevitably arise on all sets. Workdays can and frequently do last from fourteen to sixteen hours, six or seven days a week. This situation prevails for as long as it takes to complete a project, which can be as little as a few weeks and as long as several months or even a year or more.

The settings in which film directors work naturally vary, depending on where the project is made. Much television and movie work happens on a soundstage, typically a large building with high ceilings to accommodate sets and large overhead lighting grids. Shooting can also take place on location. In that case, directors can find themselves working almost anywhere in the world.

Earnings

Because of their importance in the entertainment industry, directors are among the best paid of all filmmakers. Their salary can vary, depending on factors such as the type of project (for example, a feature film versus a TV commercial), the length of the production schedule, and whether the project is union or non-

With help from the scriptwriter, a director records a scene from their movie. After the production phase is complete, the director will oversee work by the film editor, music scorer, and others who help transform the work into a finished film.

union. A nonunion project always pays less to everyone involved, including the director.

In general, most professional directors make several hundred dollars a day or a few thousand dollars per week for a small project such as a commercial or a half-hour TV episode. Hour-long TV shows and low-budget feature films pay more, and big-budget features pay even more. A union director working on a feature film usually makes from $3,000 to $5,000 per day, an arrangement that generally lasts for as long as the project is in production. Sometimes, however, a director may negotiate a contract in which he or she makes little or nothing up front and relies instead on earning a percentage of the project's profits.

Still another crucial factor that determines a director's earnings is his or her track record and reputation. A handful of famous directors can command fees in excess of $10 million. Members of that exclusive club include the likes of James Cameron, Ridley Scott, and Steven Spielberg. Scott made an estimated $10 million to $12 million for directing *Alien: Covenant* (2017).

Opportunities for Advancement

Most of the time directors advance in the film industry in one of two ways. They might transition from making small-scale projects to larger ones, as when Scott made the leap from TV commercials to feature films. More commonly they increase their value as directors by turning out profitable films. For example, director Patty Jenkins made about $1 million to direct *Wonder Woman* (2017). Because the movie did well at the box office, she made more than $8 million to direct the sequel, making her the highest-paid woman director up to that time.

What Is the Future Outlook for Film and TV Directors?

According to industry analysts and the Bureau of Labor Statistics, the need for directors will increase considerably in the 2020s, with a possible growth rate of 12 percent or more. This is expected to stem from a strong public demand for more movies and TV shows, along with more foreign demand to see American-made films.

Find Out More

Academy of Motion Picture Arts and Sciences
8949 Wilshire Blvd.
Beverly Hills, CA 90211
website: www.oscars.org

The Academy of Motion Picture Arts and Sciences is dedicated to promoting excellence and opportunity for artists in filmmaking at all levels, including directors. Its comprehensive website features information about student fellowships in directing and the special Oscars awarded each year to student directors and other young filmmakers.

Directors Guild of America (DGA)
7920 Sunset Blvd.
Los Angeles, CA 90046
website: www.dga.org

The DGA is a labor organization that represents the creative and economic rights of film directors. Its website offers valuable information on film schools that offer degrees in directing, other kinds of training programs for aspiring directors, and advice on how a new director can get an agent to represent him or her.

Independent Filmmaker Project (IFP)
30 John St., Ground Floor
Brooklyn, NY 11201
website: www.ifp.org

The IFP works with independent film artists, including directors, across the world. Its website explains how the organization supports independent directors find both funding and expert advisers. In this manner, the IFP helps independent directors and other filmmakers, most of them young and aspiring, to make around 350 projects yearly.

Film and TV Production Designer

What Does a Film and TV Production Designer Do?

A production designer, sometimes called an art director in the film and television industry, is responsible for the overall look of a film or TV project. "The production designer leads the art department and oversees the visuals of the film," explains production designer Prerna Chawla in an article for the website Careers in Film. The designer of *Shooting in Vain* (2018), she states that production designers "participate in location scouting and design atmospheres that reflect the intentions and lives of the film's characters."

Usually, production designers are active mostly during the preproduction phase of a film project. However, sometimes they are needed to scout extra locations or refurbish one or more sets during the shooting phase. Early on, designers read the script and meet with the director, beginning an artistic collaboration. Designers also meet with the producer,

At a Glance

Film and TV Production Designer

Minimum Educational Requirements
None

Personal Qualities
A high degree of creativity, good drawing skills, mastery of current computer drawing and production design software

Working Conditions
Some design work done at home, sets constructed in a studio, traveling far and wide for location scouting

Salary Range
From $50,000 to $300,000

Number of Jobs
About 2,500

Future Job Outlook
Growth of 7 to 9 percent through 2024

who assigns them a budget with which to hire assistants and buy and construct the sets. Next comes research into the time period portrayed in the film and the look of the sets and initial scouted locations. "I needed to find the kind of run-down, seedy areas of the city where the little con-man, Ratso, would normally hang out," said the late production designer John Robert Lloyd in a private, previously unpublished interview given in 1969. He was describing his location scouting for *Midnight Cowboy* (1969), which won the Oscar for best motion picture. "We used those places for exterior establishing shots, mainly. Most of the interiors were sets built on the sound stage. It would have been too difficult and expensive to get electricity into the abandoned buildings, light them, and then cart in an entire film crew and all that heavy equipment."

In fact, designing and constructing sets is one of the chief duties of film and TV production designers. After the basic walls and ceilings (if any) are up, the set must be dressed, and production designers oversee the set decorators they have hired to do that job. They add furniture, window drapery, wall hangings, carpets, knickknacks, and other furnishings that will make the set look like a real room in a real house or other structure. In an interview for the website for *India Today*, up-and-coming production designer Aashrita Kamath (*Kong: Skull Island*) says, "We make sure that the design of the sets, choice of locations, design of props, and everything down to the smallest detail is in keeping with the style of the film, and is appropriate for the characters."

How Do You Become a Film and TV Production Designer?

Education

Although it is not mandatory for a prospective production designer to major in art direction/production design in college, many who desire to work in that profession do attend four-year schools that offer majors in theater or art and design. Some of the best programs of that kind can be found at Carnegie Mellon University in Pittsburgh, Pennsylvania; Syracuse University in Syracuse, New

York; and the Yale School of Drama in New Haven, Connecticut. Students can get basic knowledge and some limited but valuable hands-on experience by attending such schools.

Even if these students more generally major in theater or art and design, those fields can also provide a solid foundation for specializing in set design later. Once they have gotten some experience in theater or art, it is possible to advance into set design when the proper opportunity arises. Dave Arrowsmith, the production designer for the lavish 2019 TV series *Whiskey Cavalier*, recalls in an interview for the website Vimeo that he studied art and design in college, and when the right opportunity arose to work in television, he seized it.

Today some production designers get their start by becoming apprentices, interns, or production assistants to a theatrical or film designer. After they learn the basics, the boss may let them contribute small-scale design ideas, and over time they may take on increasing responsibilities. Eventually, they may have enough experience to apply for design jobs of their own.

Volunteer Work and Internships

The available internships in set decoration and production design are most often entry-level, unpaid positions. Across the country a number of small video and film companies, along with a few larger film companies, offer such internships, including New Sky Pictures in Austin, Texas. Interns usually do all sorts of general, menial tasks and rarely do any actual designing on their own. But they may gain valuable experience by helping build and paint sets for professional designers. Interns/apprentices should always take photos of any sets they work on. These can be used to begin building a portfolio to eventually show film and TV producers.

Skills and Personality

The single most important skill that production designers must have is creativity, or put another way, artistic imagination. Designers must be able to conjure up a vision of most aspects of a finished setting and be able to employ wood, plaster, canvas, plastic, cloth, tiles, paint, and all sorts of other materials to translate that set into physical reality. In addition, the designer must be adept at technical drawing because he or she first sketches the set designs on paper to show the director.

In recent years a good deal of this artistic work has been done on computer screens, and production designers should have a working knowledge of the latest available design software. Once the director approves the designs, they become the blueprints for the construction crew and set decorators. Designers should also have extensive knowledge of historical styles of architecture, furniture, costumes, and other visual design elements and be able to quickly but accurately research those elements they are not familiar with.

Production designers should have good communication skills as well, since they always work closely with producers, directors, set decorators, and costume designers. Indeed, Chawla points out, often talent alone is not enough for an individual to achieve success in the highly competitive field of production design. Designers should also have a personality that displays likability and a sincere trust in the ideas and work of assistants and other coworkers. Chawla says,

> Production designers may try to do everything themselves but mentalities like that will only cripple a production. Adapting to new situations, discovering the opportunities built into problems, and trusting the crew are all great qualities to have. They are essential to being a production designer.

Thus, production designers should not be haughty, aloof, or unwilling to give others the respect and credit that is due them.

On the Job

Employers

Production designers work not only on feature films and television shows but also on short film subjects, TV commercials, music videos, and where appropriate, video games with filmic content.

They are employed by major studios and companies connected to those studios.

Working Conditions

Like many people who work in the film and television industry, production designers are freelance. That is, designers work for themselves. They sign a contract for each specific film project that interests them, and then they must meet a production deadline. They make their own hours, but because of the struggle to make deadlines, those hours are almost always long. "Most days are hard work that lasts at least twelve hours," Chawla says. "Work weeks are five or six days long." So it's a good idea "to try and take about a week-long break between projects to rest up or else [you will] burn out."

Moreover, there are no fixed or regular working hours for production designers. The designer's schedule can vary a lot, depending on factors such as the size of the project and design budget, the number of assistants the designer has, and the number of shooting delays and budget overruns that may occur during preproduction and shooting. As a result, production designers often have to work during evenings and/or on weekends.

Most of a production designer's initial work occurs at home, at a drafting table and computer, where the designs first come to life. Much of rest of the work takes place on sound stages in studios, where a majority of the sets are constructed. Nevertheless, travel is frequently required, sometimes involving location scouting in the United States and at other times traveling abroad if and when the movie or TV show is shot in a foreign country.

Earnings

Like music scorers and directors, production designers usually do not have fixed salaries but rather make varying amounts of money based on their level of experience, list of credits, and reputation. Another factor that affects designers' earnings is how many projects they do in a given year. Someone who does three or four projects in a row with little rest in between will obviously make more than someone who does only one project and then is out of work for several months.

Thus, film and TV production designers who work only sporadically make as little as $50,000 to $70,000 a year, while busier ones can make $130,000 to $140,000 or more annually. The few who have designed one or more big-budget movies can make quite a bit more—$300,000 or more. At the top of the heap are the production designers of most of the films that cost more than $200 million to make—including *Transformers: Age of Extinction* (2014), *Jurassic World* (2015), and *Justice League* (2017)—who earned more than $700,000 each.

Opportunities for Advancement

Beginning production designers who land small-scale jobs such as TV commercials, music videos, and an occasional single TV episode generally attempt to advance by obtaining both more frequent work and bigger-budget projects. Little-known designers will therefore sometimes try to get gigs in which they design most or all of the episodes of a popular television series. For example, the great modern production designer Gemma Jackson did several TV series before moving slowly into feature films, including *Bridget Jones's Diary* (2001). Later, she went back to television, this time with a much larger budget, to do one of the most popular TV series in the world, *Game of Thrones*.

> ## What Is the Future Outlook for Film and TV Production Designers?

Partly because production design is such a specialized field that takes considerable time and effort to break into, the number of new designers who enter the profession each year is fairly minimal. Moreover, although the number of feature films and TV shows made each year is steadily increasing, many of the production design jobs in new ones are scooped up by established designers who have done only one or two jobs per year in the past. As a result, the number of new production designers needed throughout most of the 2020s is expected to be minimal—only a few hundred per year. This suggests that competition for production designer jobs will remain very strong for some time to come.

Find Out More

Art Directors Guild (ADG)
11969 Ventura Blvd.
Studio City, CA 91604
website: https://adg.org

The ADG provides mentorship, supervision, and on-the-job training for future production designers/art directors. The organization's website explains how young prospective designers can sign up for the training and describes the courses available. Part of the training involves working on design projects that give the participants hands-on experience.

Independent Filmmaker Project (IFP)
30 John St., Ground Floor
Brooklyn, NY 11201
website: www.ifp.org

The IFP works with independent film artists, including production designers and art directors, in the United States, Canada, and other counties. Its website features descriptions of the organization's efforts to provide funding and advice for talented people who are new to the film business. Young production designers can get valuable experience this way.

Set Decorators Society of America (SDSA)
7100 Tujunga Ave., Suite A
North Hollywood, CA 91605
website: www.setdecorators.org

The SDSA promotes high standards of excellence in production design. Its website contains a section on set design and decor that shows pictures from many current movies—some big budget, others not. The images capture numerous elements of professional production design, and young aspiring designers study them to help learn the trade.

Film and TV Stuntperson

What Does a Film and TV Stuntperson Do?

Stuntpeople, sometimes called stunt performers, are actors who perform feats on film that are too risky for average actors, who lack the proper training to do them safely. Typically, stuntpeople fall off horses, moving cars, or buildings; take part in high-speed car chases; and perform realistic-looking staged fights of various kinds. On film and TV sets in which multiple stunt performers are required, one of them acts as stunt coordinator. He or she often hires the others, oversees them, and designs most of the stunts.

There are two basic types of stuntpeople or approaches to stunt work. In the first, the stuntperson is hired as an actor who has stunt training and plays a character usually seen only in the scene or scenes in which the stunts occur. In the second approach, the stunt performer is hired to double for a specific lead or featured player. In such a case the stuntperson is referred to as a stunt double. A few major lead actors—for example, Tom Cruise—prefer to do their own stunts. Sometimes they are allowed to and are paid extra

At a Glance

Film and TV Stuntperson

Minimum Educational Requirements
None

Personal Qualities
Strength, agility, athletic prowess, and strong skills in falling, climbing, swimming, car and motorcycle driving, sword fighting, and more

Working Conditions
Long hours spent either on studio sound stages or in a wide variety of outdoor locations

Salary Range
From $5,000 to $250,000 in 2018

Number of Jobs
About 400 to 500 in 2018

Future Job Outlook
Minimal growth through 2024

for it; in other cases, however, the producer forbids it, fearing that if that actor is seriously injured while doing a stunt, much money will be lost when the production shuts down to wait for him or her to recover.

One important difference between these two approaches to stunt work is that a regular stunt player can show his or her face on camera. This is because that person is playing a character who happens to fall off a horse or get into a fight. In contrast, a stunt double cannot show his or her face. Although the double will look somewhat like the actor, the resemblance will not be exact; so if the camera reveals the double's face, the illusion will be ruined. Hence, filmmakers go to great lengths to try to hide a stunt double's face in one way or another.

How Do You Become a Film and TV Stuntperson?

Education

No specific or minimum educational requirements exist for stunt-people. Many individuals who enter the profession learn by doing. That is, they often start by performing fairly simple stunts in the occasional crowd stunt scenes seen in feature films. A large-scale barroom brawl involving twenty to thirty characters or a battle scene featuring hundreds of people fighting and falling are typical examples. Over time, stuntpeople graduate to more difficult and more dangerous stunts.

Increasingly, however, prospective stunt performers try to attend one of a growing number of special schools that train stuntpeople. Perhaps the best known is the International Stunt School in Washington State. One can also offer to pay for in-dividual tutoring by an established stuntperson. "If you can," says American stunt coordinator Gregg Sargeant in an article for *Backstage* magazine online, "seek out an instructor who's a working Hollywood stunt professional, as they're respected as the best in the world."

Still other would-be stunt performers take a more general route by majoring in theater in a college or private dramatics academy.

There, if they have gymnastics or judo training or some equivalent, they can distinguish themselves by volunteering to do spectacular falls and other stunts that other student performers would not dare to attempt. Later, they can audition to act in low-budget films, join the Screen Actors Guild (SAG), and hopefully display their stunt skills when an opportunity arises. That is how stuntwoman April Sutton got her big break. She was working as an extra on the set of a television series at the time. Near the end of the shoot, she recalls in an interview for *Cosmopolitan* magazine,

> one of the stunt coordinators said there was an opportunity to do a stunt. I would play a guard who gets shot, and I would need to do a reaction move where I whip around and fall on my back. He asked me to try it right there on the spot. I gave it a shot, and I was hired.

Whatever approach to the business they may employ, prospective stuntpeople should get into and remain in top physical condition. They should also relentlessly train in tumbling, wrestling, boxing, gymnastics, horseback riding, dancing, rock climbing, sword fighting, and other similar disciplines. In an interview on the website Vimeo, Jessica Erin Bennett, a stunt performer for *The Walking Dead*, says "the more well-rounded you are, the better."

Volunteer Work and Internships

Apprenticeships and internships in stunt work are very hard to come by. But if a would-be stuntperson is both unusually talented and hardworking, he or she may be able to train with a professional stunt performer, either in a school setting or in individual tutoring. The student may, in exceptional cases, become a sort of apprentice who steadily moves into professional situations by working with the teacher.

Skills and Personality

Stuntpeople invariably possess a number of specialized, often impressive physical skills. These include the ability to fall from various heights and not get seriously hurt, yet make it look like they were killed or badly injured; or similarly, to both throw and receive fake but realistic-looking punches and kicks. In addition to the strength and agility required for such moves, a modern stuntperson should be able to maneuver a car or motorcycle at high speeds; ride and fall from a galloping horse; climb a sheer, vertical rock wall; swim, dive, and use scuba equipment; load and fire guns of various kinds; and fight with diverse types of swords. Some stunt performers are known for specializing in one or more of these areas.

Noted stuntman Eddie Braun advocates in a *Backstage* article that stunt performers should also display strong people skills, including having impeccable manners and an overtly friendly personality. The reason, he says, is that finding work frequently necessitates having meetings with producers and directors, who are used to dealing with professionals armed with good social skills.

Many of the skills a stuntperson needs, Bennett points out, come from experience. Yet, she adds, one can get a jump along the learning curve by doing one's homework. Part of that, she says, consists of watching classic movies containing famous or difficult stunts and watching the stunt performers' styles, techniques, and timing. Also, she recommends reading books such as Mollie Gregory's *Stuntwomen: The Untold Hollywood Story* and Kevin Conley's *The Full Burn*.

On the Job

Employers
The majority of stuntpeople are freelancers who contract with individual film and TV productions on a job-by-job basis. But a few acting jobs involving stunt work can be found in theme parks, such as Universal Studios in Orlando, Florida; circuses; and other live shows.

Working Conditions
Stuntpeople almost always work long hours during a given day of shooting. Fourteen- or fifteen-hour days are not unusual. Moreover, the physical conditions for a stunt performer can be

extremely uncomfortable. Consider, for instance, the plight of a stuntperson who is partially submerged in cold water for hours at a time, as was the case for many stunt performers who worked on James Cameron's epic film *Titanic*. It is also not uncommon for stuntpeople to work in hot desert conditions or to perform repeated falls onto hard concrete sidewalks.

Some stunt work takes place on sound stages in studios; just as often the shoot takes place outside in one of countless diverse settings, from city streets to forests to beaches to mountainsides. Wherever the work may be located, writes stunt performer Cori Hundt (in his online article "How to Become a Stuntperson"), "as a stunt performer, just like any other performer on set, you will essentially be told to 'hurry up and wait.' This means you might be on set anywhere from eight to 20 hours at a time, but only filming for a small portion of that." Thus, working as a stuntperson on a movie set is not mostly an adventurous and fun experience, as some aspiring stunt performers imagine. It is very hard and at times tedious work.

Earnings
The amount of money stuntpeople make depends on factors such as how often they find work, their level of experience and reputations, and the difficulty of the stunts they perform. Even if they belong to SAG, as most stuntpeople do, stunt performers who work on a two- or three-day shoot only once in a year will likely make little more than $5,000. In contrast, a stuntperson who gets one gig after another for months on end might make well over $100,000 in a year. Around $70,000 is the average annual earnings of a reasonably busy stunt performer. Nevertheless, a handful of top-tier performers who have major reputations in the business can make as much as $250,000 or more per year.

Opportunities for Advancement
The main way that stuntpeople advance their careers is by getting more and more work; the primary way to do that is to network whenever possible. While spending long hours on a set, a stunt professional should try to get to know as many actors and crew

members as possible. The idea is that at least some of them will remember him or her and later may be in a position to recommend the person for a job in a future shoot.

In addition, a few stuntpeople manage to advance by becoming well-known actors. Burt Reynolds, Jackie Chan, and Chuck Norris are among the former stuntmen who became A-list actors. One other possible way for stunt performers to better themselves is by transitioning from performers into teachers and crew members. "I am excited," April Sutton remarks, about "building my personal training business to work with more actors and actresses. My goal is to open my own private studio in Chicago. I think I have a good 10 years before my body gets tired. I do think about what's next, and I've always felt that I could work behind the camera as a stunt coordinator, or a director, writer, or producer."

What Is the Future Outlook for Film and TV Stuntpeople?

Although several thousand stunt performers belong to SAG, only a small percentage of them work all year long, and some are lucky to land one well-paying gig per year. As a result, many have second jobs to make ends meet. Industry analysists expect that situation to continue in the 2020s. Like other people who work in movies and television, someone who wants to work as a stuntperson will find the job search to be challenging. First and foremost, it requires talent. But getting work as a stuntperson will also require dedication, perseverance, lots of networking, and a healthy dose of old-fashioned good luck.

Find Out More

International Stunt School
PO Box 80084
Seattle, WA 98108
website: www.stuntschool.com

The International Stunt School is regarded by a majority of stunt professionals as the best overall stunt training program in North America. The group's website contains information about the newest seasonal training sessions and how to apply. It also lists Hollywood casting representatives who visit the school each year and explains how students can meet them.

Screen Actors Guild/American Federation of
Television and Radio Artists (SAG-AFTRA)
5757 Wilshire Blvd., Seventh Floor
Los Angeles, CA 90036
website: www.sagaftra.org

SAG-AFTRA brings together two great American labor unions: the Screen Actors Guild and the American Federation of Television and Radio Artists. Members include actors, dancers, singers, and stunt performers. The wide-ranging SAG-AFTRA website contains helpful information about how young performers can get started in the film and television industries.

Stuntwomen's Association of Motion Pictures
website: https://stuntwomen.com

Founded in 1967, the Stuntwomen's Association of Motion Pictures represents trained female professional stunt performers. Its website contains photos of all forty-two members, plus a gallery of those members who regularly double for well-known actresses. There are also excellent detailed descriptions of the main kinds of stunt work, which aspiring stuntpeople will find helpful.

Interview with a Director

Film and TV director, producer, and special effects supervisor George Bloom has worked for Walt Disney Studios, CBS, and other major entertainment companies and was nominated for an Emmy for directing the virtual reality version of the popular Netflix series *Stranger Things*. He has also directed more than eighty TV commercials and many music videos, including ones for Ringo Starr and the Stone Temple Pilots. He answered questions about his career in an interview with the author conducted by email.

Q: Why and how did you become a film and TV director?
A: I first enjoyed expressing myself with a still camera as a young man. Capturing an image was an expressive experience, and I migrated that interest into buying a film camera and shooting all sorts of things I saw around me. I later decided to attend film school at the Brooks Institute, which had a small film production program. It was there that I started to film short subjects and learn how to communicate a message through film. Not long afterward I was lucky to land a job at Capitol Records during the birth of music videos. It was there that I directed music videos for many artists, and thus began a 15 year career as a director in commercials, product promos, music videos, and one movie.

Q: Can you describe your typical workday?
A: You are part of a small army of creative people, and the actual time you spend directing is small. But the role of the director is not only guiding the performance of a scene or individual camera

shot, it is also communicating to people in all the departments on your team what you want. It is imperative that the whole group is in sync with your personal vision. A typical day consists of the lighting set up, making sure all props are in place, seeing that the actors are in makeup, making sure the camera department is readying the shots, and, depending on the type of production, you either have story boards or a good plan for how you will execute your scenes that day. When the plan is ready, you disseminate it to your team. For example: If you have a 10 hour shooting day, you might actually direct for only 3 hours in that time span, so you need to be ready and prepared for unexpected problems you might have to solve.

Q: What do you like most and least about your job?
A: The amount of time you must spend on the set actually physically directing actors in specific scenes takes up just a small part of the day. The rest of the time you're waiting for your crew of 40+ people to organize and prepare for each shot or scene. Meanwhile, as the chief planner of all that activity, you are making small incremental steps in making the overall film, sort of like climbing a mountain step by step to eventually get to the top. It is a game of patience and persistence to insure you get what you want out of the actors and crew.

Q: What personal qualities do you find most valuable for this type of work?
A: You must have a vision of what you want and develop that with the other members of your team and let everyone express themselves in a small way to help rally your vision. It is not about being a dictator, but rather about being a collaborator and surrounding yourself with others who have ideas or options to select from, all of which build on and enhance your own work. Extremely important is to be well read about filmmaking, and to have the ability to tell a story well and get across to the viewers the core emotional spine of what you're trying to communicate. In a sense, you are your own therapist, who explores in a deep way what you really want to communicate in this or that moment.

Q: What advice do you have for students who might be interested in this career?

A: I started out in music videos and commercials and soon realized that those areas are very much director-driven forms of media. The director is king and gives the vision and really guides the whole essence of the finished material. However, when you move into television, the director sometimes plays second fiddle, so to speak. He or she is less important than the script itself, which is king, and the director merely helps lay out the shots for the actors to express the scene. In many TV series the actors know more about their character than you, the guest director, so you're more of a shepherd.

Other Jobs in Film, TV, and Theater

Actor
ADR recordist
Animal trainer
Animator
Assistant director
Boom operator
Camera operator
Casting director
Choreographer
Cinematographer
Colorist
Computer effects technician
Construction coordinator
Dialect coach
Film editor
Foley artist
Gaffer
Grip
Hairdresser
Jimmy-jib operator
Line producer
Location manager
Marketing/publicity director
Master carpenter
Master electrician

Master painter
Matte painter
Motion graphics designer
Music editor
Playwright
Postproduction supervisor
Producer
Production accountant
Production assistant
Prop master
Rerecording mixer
Screenwriter
Script supervisor
Set decorator
Sound engineer
Sound mixer
Special effects editor
Special effects supervisor
Stage manager
Steadicam operator
Storyboard artist
Titles designer
Travel coordinator
Videographer
Voice-over artist

Editor's note: The US Department of Labor's Bureau of Labor Statistics provides information about hundreds of occupations. The agency's *Occupational Outlook Handbook* describes what these jobs entail, the work environment, education and skill requirements, pay, future outlook, and more. The *Occupational Outlook Handbook* may be accessed online at www.bls.gov/ooh.

Index

Picture Credits

About the Author

In addition to his numerous acclaimed volumes on ancient civilizations, historian Don Nardo has published several studies of current social, economic, and scientific issues, including *Debates on LGBT Issues*, *The Women's Movement*, *How Vaccines Changed the World*, *Climate Change*, *Nanotechnology and Medicine*, *Careers in Education*, and award-winning books on space exploration. Nardo also composes and arranges orchestral music. He lives with his wife, Christine, in Massachusetts.